Keeping Unusual Pets

Chinchillas

Tom Handford

Chicago, Illinois

www.heinemannraintree.com
Visit our website to find out more information about Heinemann-Raintree books.

To order:
☎ Phone 888-454-2279
💻 Visit www.heinemannraintree.com to browse our catalog and order online.

© 2002, 2010 Heinemann Library
an imprint of Capstone Global Library, LLC
Chicago, Illinois

Edited by Louise Galpine, Megan Cotugno, and Laura Knowles
Designed by Kim Miracle and Victoria Bevan
Picture research by Mica Brancic
Originated by Capstone Global Library Ltd 2010
Printed and bound in China by Leo Paper Products Ltd

14 13 12 11 10
10 9 8 7 6 5 4 3 2 1

Library of Congress Cataloging-in-Publication Data
Handford, Tom, 1938-
  Chinchillas / Tom Handford. -- 2nd ed.
    p. cm. -- (Keeping unusual pets)
  Includes bibliographical references and index.
  ISBN 978-1-4329-3852-9
  1. Chinchillas as pets--Juvenile literature. I. Title.
  SF459.C48H36 2010
  636.935'93--dc22

                        2009035286

Acknowledgments
The author and publisher are grateful to the following for permission to reproduce copyright material: Alamy pp. **10** (© Juniors Bildarchiv), **44 right middle** (© Ben Molyneux People), **44 top** (© Alan J. Jones); © Capstone Global Library pp. **5, 6, 7, 7 top, 9 top, 9 bottom, 11 top, 11 bottom, 12, 13, 15, 16, 17, 18 top, 18 bottom, 19, 21, 22, 23, 24, 25, 26 top, 26 bottom, 27, 28, 29 top, 30 top, 30 bottom, 31, 32, 34, 35 top, 35 bottom, 36 top, 36 bottom, 37, 38, 39, 42, 43** (Tudor Photography); © Capstone Publishers pp. **14, 29 bottom, 33 top, 33 bottom, 40, 41** (Karon Dubke); iStockphoto p. **4** (© Jameson Weston); Nature Picture Library pp. **8 bottom** (© Steimer/ARCO), **45** (© Ulrike Schanz); NHPA p. **8 top** (© Tom Handford); Photolibrary p. **20** (© Juniors Bildarchiv); Science Photo Library p. **44 left** (© Carolyn A. McKeone).

Cover photograph of a young chinchilla reproduced with permission of Shutterstock (© Eric Isselée).

We would like to thank Judy Tuma and Rob Lee for their invaluable help in the preparation of this book.

Contents

Any words appearing in the text in bold, **like this**, are explained in the glossary.

What Is a Chinchilla?

Chinchillas are small animals with very soft, dense fur that gives them a plump appearance. They are **mammals**, which means they are **warm-blooded** (they produce their own body heat), give birth to live babies, and feed their babies with their milk. Chinchillas are members of the **rodent** family, which includes rats and mice. Rodents have very sharp front teeth for gnawing at their food.

DID YOU KNOW?

✪ Children are not allowed to buy pets themselves. You should always have an adult with you when you buy your pet.

✪ Chinchillas are named after the Chincha people, a native tribe of the Andes Mountains in South America, where chinchillas are found. *Chinchilla* means "little Chincha."

Chinchillas have very long whiskers, a curly, bushy tail, and powerful back legs for hopping and jumping. They use their short front paws to hold their food.

Chinchillas under threat

A wild chinchilla's first defense from a predator, such as a fox or eagle, is to flee. Sometimes they stand on their hind legs to seem larger, bare their sharp teeth, and make sounds. A chinchilla might also spray **urine** at a predator.

A chinchilla's deep fur protects, too, because a predator needs to take a very big bite to catch more than a mouthful of fur! The fur keeps chinchillas warm in the cold mountains. It also prevents water from evaporating from their bodies. They can move quickly on rocks with their padded feet.

Wild chinchillas eat grasses and other vegetation. Morning dew and cacti provide them with water in their dry habitats.

In the 1700s chinchilla fur became fashionable in Europe. So many were killed for their fur that in the 1800s governments established rules against trapping and killing chinchillas. Unfortunately, some hunting and trapping still takes place.

The chinchillas' habitat also continues to shrink because of the expansion of mining, wood collection, and grazing livestock. Habitat conservation projects are underway in Chile, the only country where wild chinchillas live today.

Like most chinchillas sold around the world today, this chinchilla is descended from just 12 animals that were brought into the United States in 1923.

Chinchilla Facts

Pet chinchillas are different from their wild cousins. For one thing, they are usually larger—a fully grown adult male or female pet chinchilla weighs from 450 to 1,150 grams (1 to 2½ pounds) and is about the size of a small rabbit. Female chinchillas are usually larger than males. Pet chinchillas have fur that comes in a variety of colors.

AMAZING COLORS

- ✪ Nearly all wild chinchillas are gray.

- ✪ There are now over 20 different colors of pet chinchilla because of **selective breeding**.

- ✪ Gray pet chinchillas are known as "standard" chinchillas.

- ✪ Experts have special names for pet chinchillas' colors, such as sapphire, black velvet, brown velvet, violet, pink white, and royal blue.

The picture below shows a standard (gray) chinchilla and a pink white chinchilla.

Nighttime fun

Chinchillas are **nocturnal** animals, which means that most of their activities take place at night. They race around the walls of their cage and play with pieces of wood and other objects in their cage. Chinchillas may wake up for short periods of time during their normal daytime sleep.

This picture shows (from left to right) a *self black*, a *pink white*, a *standard*, and a *Wilson white* chinchilla.

DID YOU KNOW?

❂ Some chinchillas may live for up to 20 years. The average life span for a well-cared-for pet is 12 to 15 years.

❂ Chinchillas make a lot of different sounds to show their feelings, including chirps, squeaks, and barks.

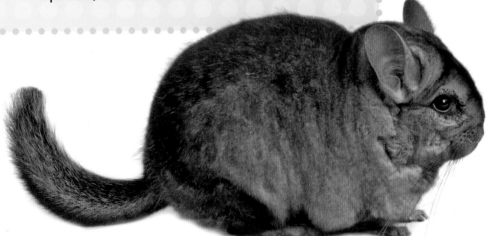

Chinchilla babies

Female chinchillas are pregnant for 111 to 125 days and can give birth twice a year. Baby chinchillas are called **kits**. There can be one, two, or three kits in each **litter**. When they are first born, the kits weigh between 25 and 50 grams (0.9 and 1.8 ounces).

This chinchilla kit is only a few minutes old. When they are born, baby chinchillas are very wet and soon get cold. They creep under their mother, whose body heat helps to dry them.

DID YOU KNOW?

✪ Kits are born with fur and their eyes open.

✪ A few hours after they are born, they are able to walk, see, and hear.

✪ After one day they can run around their cage.

✪ Kits spend a lot of time suckling (drinking milk) from their mother.

✪ A suckling kit can sometimes injure its mother by biting her.

This kit is a few days old. It is covered in soft baby fur and is busy suckling milk from its mother.

Weaning

When they are about eight weeks old, baby kits stop **suckling** from their mother and start to eat solid food. This is called **weaning**. After weaning, pet chinchilla kits start eating pellets and hay. At this age, they are independent of their mother and can take care of themselves.

When kits are weaned, they will eat solid food and can survive without their mother.

This one-year-old chinchilla is fully grown and has its adult fur.

Is a Chinchilla for You?

Chinchillas look beautiful and are a lot of fun to play with, but they need to be taken care of every day. Your pet chinchilla will be your friend if you treat it kindly and tend to all its needs, but if you are rough with it, treat it unkindly, or frighten it, your chinchilla will nip or bite you. A female chinchilla will also spray you with her **urine** if you upset her. This is the way that chinchillas protect themselves. It should not happen if you treat your chinchilla kindly. The more attention you give to your pet, the more pleasure and fun it will give back to you.

GOOD POINTS

✪ Chinchillas are easy to care for and they usually stay healthy.

✪ They are sturdy little creatures that usually live for a long time.

✪ They are not expensive to feed.

✪ There are many colors of chinchilla to choose from.

✪ Chinchillas do not have a smell.

✪ Fleas and other insects cannot live in a chinchilla's fur because it is so dense.

✪ Normally, chinchillas will not bite you if they like you and you pick them up properly.

Chinchilla fur is very soft to touch. They keep it clean by **grooming** themselves.

NOT-SO-GOOD POINTS

✪ You cannot take a chinchilla for a walk, as you can a dog or even a ferret.

✪ You cannot let chinchillas loose in the yard.

✪ If you let chinchillas run around a chinchilla-safe room, you will find droppings wherever they go. However, these droppings are very dry and are easy to clean up.

✪ Chinchillas need larger cages than smaller **rodents**, such as hamsters or mice.

✪ Chinchillas love to gnaw things, so you will need to watch out for your furniture and other objects!

✪ Some people have an **allergy** to chinchilla fur.

A chinchilla can make an excellent pet, but you cannot leave it to roam around your house like you might a cat or a dog.

Yes or no?

Having a chinchilla for a pet means caring for it every day and always treating it with respect. Think this over carefully before you make the decision to become a chinchilla owner.

Chinchillas will gnaw at anything! If you let your pet run free in a room, you must watch it all the time and keep it from chewing on precious things or things that might be bad for it.

Choosing a Chinchilla

You can adopt a chinchilla from some animal shelters, or you can buy one from your local pet store or from a **breeder.** You can also look on the Internet for your local chinchilla club or group. The people at local chinchilla groups will be able to give you useful information about where to buy chinchillas.

Which one?

• Try to buy a chinchilla that is 12 to 16 weeks old. Young chinchillas will quickly learn to trust you.

• Both male and female chinchillas make good pets.

• Standard gray chinchillas are cheaper than colored chinchillas.

• Do not rush into buying a chinchilla. It is better to wait until you find an animal that is perfect for you in every way.

Always ask to hold the chinchilla you would like to buy. If it is relaxed and friendly, it should be a good pet for you.

TOP TIP

Make sure the chinchilla that you choose does not chew its fur. A chinchilla with patches of very short, chewed fur will not make a good pet. It will always be very nervous and never look as beautiful as one with perfect fur.

Tooth problems

Look very carefully at your chinchilla's teeth to check that they are straight and not **overgrown**. Ask the pet store owner or chinchilla breeder to check the chinchilla's teeth for **malocclusion**. Chinchillas suffering from this condition have teeth that grow too long and are bent or **deformed**.

WHAT TO LOOK FOR

There are a few basic things to look out for when you are choosing your chinchilla.

✪ The chinchilla should be living in clean surroundings.

✪ Its eyes, nose, and ears should be clean and free from **discharge**.

✪ Its fur should be very thick, fluffy, and shiny. There should be no mats or bare patches.

✪ Its teeth should be a yellow-orange color and should not be crooked or overgrown.

✪ Select a chinchilla that is curious about you. It may come to sniff your hand.

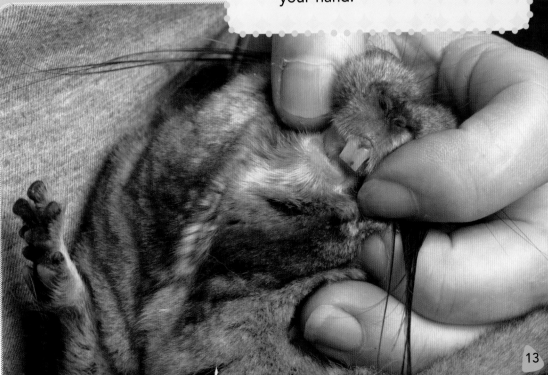

This chinchilla has good teeth that are the right color and length and are nice and straight.

One chinchilla or two?

Should you have just one chinchilla or a pair? The answer to this question is up to you and your family. Many people have only one chinchilla, and both the pet and its owners seem happy with this arrangement. If you have never owned a chinchilla before, it is probably best to start with just one.

If you do decide to have two chinchillas, here are some things to think about:

• Make sure you have a cage that is big enough for two animals to live in comfortably.

• It is best to buy two males or two females.

• When you are choosing your male or female pair, try to buy brothers or sisters. They will be used to living together and should be happy to share a cage.

• If you keep a male and female together, they will probably **breed** and have young. Caring for baby chinchillas is a big task that should only be undertaken by experienced chinchilla owners.

Your new pets may have been in the same cage before you bought them. However, when you put them in your cage, stay with them until you are sure that they feel safe in their new home.

It is best to introduce two animals in the morning, because this is the time when they are sleepy and not very active.

Introducing chinchillas

It is possible for two chinchillas to live together happily, but they may take a while to settle down. If the animals were in separate cages before you bought them, be very careful when you introduce them for the first time. They might fight. One way to do this successfully is to put the two animals in separate cages side by side, about 5 centimeters (2 inches) apart. That way they can smell and see each other, but cannot fight or get hurt. After seven days, the animals will have gotten to know one another. Now you can put the two animals into one cage. Always try to introduce them in a cage that neither of them has been in before.

If the pair start to fight, put them back into their own cages right away. Then try to introduce them again another time. If they continue to fight, you should talk to a shelter, pet store, or a chinchilla breeder about finding a new home for one of them.

TAKE IT SLOWLY

Never hurry or be impatient when introducing chinchillas for the first time. If they do not get along, they might fight and even kill each other.

Your Chinchilla's Home

You will need the right cage and equipment to keep your chinchilla happy and healthy. You can buy a cage at a pet store or from a supplier of chinchilla equipment. Try looking on the Internet for suppliers of cages and equipment or contact your local chinchilla group (see page 47) for help and advice.

Choosing a cage

Chinchilla cages are available in many shapes and sizes, but all good cages are made from 16-gauge quality **galvanized** (rust-proof) wire mesh. You will need to buy an all-wire cage because chinchillas have very sharp teeth and can chew through other materials. Wooden hutches and cages with plastic parts will not work.

INSIDE THE CAGE

Your cage needs:

✪ a hay rack

✪ a water bottle container

✪ a food bowl

✪ one or two wooden shelves fixed to the back or the side of the cage for your chinchilla to climb onto. Keep the shelves clean. You may need to replace them if your pet has chewed them a lot.

To keep your chinchilla healthy, you must give it a good home.

The perfect place

Your chinchilla's cage needs to be placed next to a wall or in the corner of a room. It should also be raised above the ground. The cage should not be positioned in direct sunlight or too close to a radiator because your chinchilla will get too hot.

A cage measuring 60 cm wide by 45 cm deep by 75 cm high (24 by 18 by 30 in.) would be suitable for one chinchilla. For two chinchillas you will need a cage measuring 100 cm wide by 60 cm deep by 100 cm high (40 by 24 by 40 in.). Chinchillas do not need very tall cages because they are rock hoppers rather than climbers. However, they do enjoy having plenty of space, so even if you only have one pet, buy a bigger cage if you can afford it.

TOP TIP

Never put your chinchilla's cage in the middle of a room. Your pet will not know which side of its cage you will appear from next. This will make it feel very nervous.

Food containers

Your chinchilla's food container does not need to be very big—it only has to hold a couple of tablespoons of pellets. The most important thing is that your pet should not be able to tip it over! It should either be too heavy for your pet to move or it should be held in place by a clip attached to the wall of the cage.

Many cages sold today have food containers built into them. If your food container is not built in, make sure that it is heavy so that your chinchilla cannot tip it over and spill the pellets.

When your chinchilla eats pellets, it will pick them up with its teeth but then hold them in one paw while chewing.

Water bottles

The best water container for your pet is a plastic bottle that hangs on the outside of its cage. You can buy these water bottles from pet stores. Bottles come in a variety of sizes. A 500-milliliter (16-fluid ounce) bottle should fit the clip attached to your cage.

It is not a good idea to have a water bowl inside your chinchilla's cage because the water can easily get dirty from droppings, waste food, or **urine**. Dirty water can make your pet very sick.

Chinchillas love to chew, so some protection around the water bottle is essential. If your cage does not have a wire holder for the bottle, put a small piece of sheet metal between the water bottle and the cage.

TOP TIP

Sometimes your pet's water bottle will get dirty inside. To clean the bottle:

- ✪ Put a little dried rice in the bottle.

- ✪ Half-fill the bottle with water.

- ✪ Place your finger or thumb over the opening and give the bottle a good shake.

- ✪ Dispose of the dirty water and rice and rinse out the bottle with clean water.

Change the water in the bottle every day. If the tap water from your home is good enough for you to drink, then it is good enough for your pet!

Dust baths

Did you know that in the wild, chinchillas take regular dust baths? They roll around in dust or sand to get their fur clean. Your chinchilla will need to take a dust bath two or three times a week to keep its fur in good condition.

Chinchillas like to take a dust bath in the evening. Let your pet bathe for about 15 minutes, then take the dust bath out of its cage.

Buying a bath

Your chinchilla's bath should be made from galvanized metal or thick glass and should be big enough for your pet to fit inside it and stretch out comfortably. You can buy a metal dust bath from a pet store or from a supplier of chinchilla equipment. Do not give your chinchilla a plastic bath because it may chew or even eat it. Plastic is very bad for chinchillas. They cannot digest it, and it can eventually kill them.

BATHING IN SAND

- Your chinchilla will need a special sort of sand made from **volcanic** mountain pumice. You can buy it from good pet stores.

- Pour about 3 centimeters (1 inch) of sand into the bottom of the bath.

- Leave your chinchilla for about 15 minutes in its bath. It will love to roll around!

- After your chinchilla has taken its bath, or if the sand is soiled, you should filter it through a very fine mesh filter.

- The filtered sand can be kept in the bath, ready for the next time.

- The bath sand can be used again and again, but you should change it every few months.

Chewing fun

Chinchillas love to chew things, and chewing helps them to wear down their teeth, which are always growing. To provide your pet with plenty of chewing exercise, you can give it small pieces of white, soft wood, such as pine. The pieces should be about 20 centimeters (8 inches) long.

Some pet stores sell special wooden blocks for chinchillas, or you could give your chinchilla a small block of apple, pear, fir, pine, or poplar wood. Ask an adult to check that the wood is pesticide free and has not been treated, glued, or painted.

Some chinchillas like to chew blocks made of a light rock called pumice stone. You can buy blocks of pumice stone from pet stores. Pumice is full of air bubbles.

Always sweep your chinchilla's droppings off chewing blocks so they do not get too dirty.

Carrying cages

A small carrying cage is a very useful piece of equipment. You can put your pet in it while you are cleaning out its regular cage or if you need to make any repairs to the cage. A carrying cage is also very useful if you need to take your pet to the vet, or if you decide to enter your pet in a chinchilla show.

This carrying cage is made of galvanized metal mesh. Carrying cages are sometimes also known as show cages because owners use them to take their pets to shows.

Sleeping boxes

Many chinchilla owners do not use sleeping boxes. If you have one you will find it harder to attract your chinchilla's attention during the day, when it is asleep in its box. However, if you do choose to have a sleeping box, make sure it is made from soft white wood, such as pine. The wood should be untreated and you should never use a plastic box. Do not forget to clean the box out every week, because in addition to sleeping in it your pet will chew away at it.

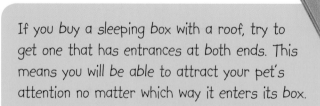

If you buy a sleeping box with a roof, try to get one that has entrances at both ends. This means you will be able to attract your pet's attention no matter which way it enters its box.

Exercise

Your chinchilla will get lots of exercise on an exercise wheel that has a solid metal running surface and attaches to the cage. This type of wheel does not have any areas where the chinchilla's tail or feet can get caught. Your chinchilla will use the walls of its cage as a racetrack and run around them very fast. It will usually exercise in the evening, when all chinchillas are wide awake.

CHINCHILLA EQUIPMENT

Here is a checklist of all the equipment that your chinchilla will need:

- ✪ metal cage with wooden shelves
- ✪ food container
- ✪ hay rack (which is usually built into the cage)
- ✪ water bottle
- ✪ dust bath
- ✪ chewing blocks
- ✪ carrying cage
- ✪ exercise wheel
- ✪ sleeping box (optional).

If possible, buy a sleeping box without a roof. Then you will be able to see your pet better!

Caring for Your Chinchilla

Caring for a pet is a big responsibility. There are some things you will need to do for your chinchilla every day.

• Feed your pet food pellets made especially for chinchillas.

• Feed your chinchilla at the same times each day. For example, feed it a few tablespoons of food pellets in the morning and a few in the evening.

• Place a handful of hay into your chinchilla's hay rack.

• Put fresh water into its water bottle.

• Play with your chinchilla for at least one hour each day.

• Always make sure your pet is healthy and happy.

Food

Give your chinchilla food pellets twice a day, in the morning and the evening. You do not need to give it very many—a few tablespoons are fine, but make sure your pet always has some pellets in its bowl. It will like to keep nibbling on them throughout the day.

Pellets made especially for chinchillas provide a balanced diet and include all the **vitamins** your pet needs. Do not feed your chinchilla any other pellets, such as rabbit or guinea pig pellets.

Chinchillas never eat a lot at once and they can waste pellets by scattering them around. If this happens, feed your chinchilla fewer pellets, but feed it more often.

Keep it simple

The only foods and liquids a chinchilla needs to stay healthy are pellets, hay, and water. Never give your pet snacks such as sunflower seeds, nuts, or chips.

Occasionally it is okay to give your chinchilla a healthy treat, such as a raisin or a very small piece of apple. But do this very rarely. It is better not to give your pet treats at all than to give it too many.

TOP TIP

Did you know that changing your chinchilla's diet from one brand of pellets to another can make it sick? Always try to buy the same brand of pellets.

VACATION CARE

- ✪ If you will be away for more than a day, it is best to ask a friend or neighbor to visit your chinchilla every day.

- ✪ Choose someone who knows and likes your chinchilla and who can be trusted to care for your pet.

- ✪ Show the person how to clean the cage, how to change the water, and how much food and hay to give your chinchilla.

- ✪ Write down all the instructions for your pet's care.

- ✪ Write down the phone number where you can be reached and your vet's phone number in case there is an emergency.

You can give your chinchilla a raisin as a very special treat, but do not give it more than one a day.

Chewing hay will keep your chinchilla happy for hours.

Fresh hay

Your chinchilla will enjoy chewing on fresh hay. The hay will give your pet the **roughage** it needs for good digestion, and it will also have lots of fun throwing the hay around!

• You can buy fresh hay at a pet store. Buy only one bag at a time.

• Every day, clear out your chinchilla's old hay and put a handful of fresh hay into its hay rack.

• Make sure that the hay you buy is dry and dust free. It should smell sweet. If it has a musty smell, do not feed it to your pet.

Cleaning the cage

It is very important to clean your chinchilla's cage, shelves, and chewing blocks every week. Cleaning out its cage is not difficult. Simply wipe over the inside and outside of the cage with warm, soapy water. Then rinse it thoroughly with clean water. Do the same for the shelves and chewing blocks if they are dirty. Make sure the cage is completely dry before you put your pet back in.

Removing waste

All chinchilla cages should have a waste tray, which fits directly underneath the cage. This is to catch all your pet's waste and droppings. Place several sheets of newspaper in the waste tray. At the end of each day, roll up the old newspaper covered in droppings and waste. Throw it away in a safe place. Replace it with several sheets of clean newspaper. If the tray is wet with **urine**, wash the tray, then rinse it and wipe it dry. Always wash your hands after cleaning your chinchilla's cage.

DO NOT SPRAY!

Never use insect sprays, spray cleaners, air fresheners, or perfume near your pets. All these products are harmful and may poison your chinchilla.

You should replace the newspaper in the bottom of the waste tray every day. Remember to wash your hands after you have done this.

27

Health checks

It is important to check your chinchilla regularly to make sure that it is healthy.

- Are your chinchilla's eyes clear?
- Does its fur look shiny and healthy?
- Does it seem bright and **alert**?

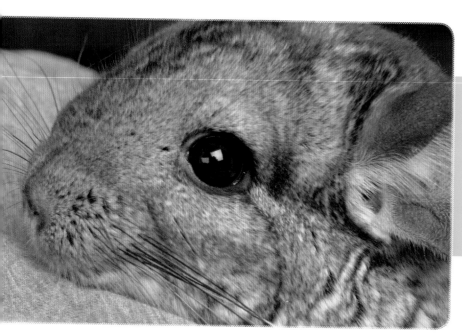

This chinchilla has bright, healthy eyes, with no redness or wet patches around them.

If your pet seems sick

If your chinchilla is sitting in the corner of its cage, being very quiet and not taking any interest in what you are doing, then something may be wrong. Make sure that your pet's pellets and water have not been soiled. Check that the droppings in the waste tray are firm and dry. If they are messy and wet, you may have fed your pet some moldy hay. Do not feed your chinchilla any hay for three to four days, and check your pet regularly to make sure that it is not getting any worse.

If your chinchilla is sick for more than a day, take it to the vet. There is more advice on chinchilla illnesses and how to treat them on pages 36–41.

These are normal chinchilla droppings. They are firm, fairly dry, and **cylindrical** in shape.

Keeping cool

Chinchillas have very thick, dense fur. In the winter this keeps them cozy and warm, but in the summer they shed some of their fur. The ideal temperature for a chinchilla is 16°Celsius (61°Fahrenheit). The temperature should never fall below the freezing point. If the temperature reaches 27°C (80°F) or higher, your chinchilla could get overheated and suffer from heatstroke. You will need to do something fast to lower the temperature. Put cold water in your chinchilla's water bottle. If the cage has a metal tray bottom, it can be set on ice packs. During very warm weather, do not handle your chinchilla.

Give your chinchilla a terracotta pot or tiles that have been chilled in the freezer to lie on. These will help keep your pet cool.

HEALTH WARNING

You will know if your pet is too warm because its ears will become bright pink or red.

Chinchilla fur

Your pet chinchilla does not need a lot of help to keep its fur in good condition. It will do this itself with dust baths. But there may be times when your chinchilla's fur does not seem to be in very good condition. For example, in the spring your chinchilla will lose some of its thick winter fur. This is known as **molting**.

Grooming your pet

When your chinchilla is molting, you may decide that it needs **grooming**. To groom your pet, you will need a strong metal comb. The type used for long-haired dogs and cats will work well. Some chinchilla owners use a special grooming comb when they are taking their animals to a show, but these combs are too sharp for normal use. Before using one of these special combs you must be taught what to do by an experienced chinchilla owner.

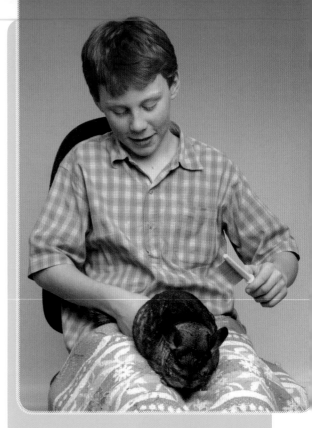

Make sure your chinchilla is happy on your lap before you start to groom it. (For more information on how to handle your chinchilla, see pages 32–33.)

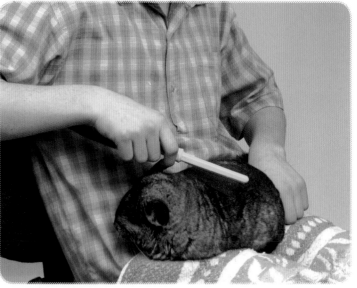

Hold your chinchilla with one hand and use your other hand to comb its fur. Always comb from head to tail.

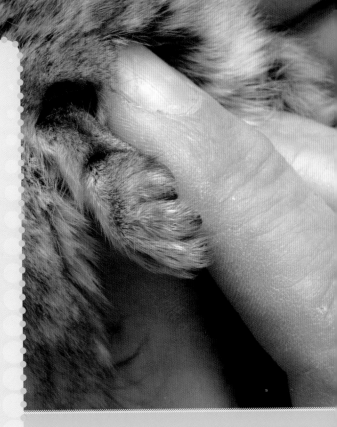

GROOMING TIPS

- ✪ Start by sitting on a chair and covering your lap with a towel or cloth.

- ✪ Place your pet on your lap and pay a lot of attention to it to gain its confidence.

- ✪ Begin grooming your chinchilla at the neck and head and work down toward the tail.

- ✪ Always comb down the body, in the direction that the fur lies.

- ✪ Remember to be patient and gentle at all times.

Chinchillas' nails do not need any attention. Your pet will keep its nails short by climbing around in its cage and playing with its pieces of wood and pumice stone.

Detaching fur

Chinchillas can detach their fur if they are grabbed suddenly. This is part of their protection system. Chinchillas living in the wild detach fur to help them escape when they are attacked by other animals or by birds of prey. They then scurry away to hide under the rocks on the mountainside. The lost fur grows back in about 10 to 12 weeks.

TOP TIP

You should never wash your chinchilla. Washing a chinchilla will cause more harm than good because it will destroy its fur's natural oils.

Handling Your Chinchilla

Making friends with your chinchilla takes time. Your pet will need to get to know you, and you will need to become confident about handling it. Remember you are like a giant to your pet! You must do everything slowly and deliberately so you do not frighten or startle it. The more you handle your pet, the more confident it will be that you will not hurt it.

Once your chinchilla feels sure you will not hurt it, it will learn to sit on your lap. Chinchillas love to sit on your lap and be tickled behind the ears. It will quickly begin to explore, and very soon it will be climbing up onto your shoulder and nibbling at you!

GAINING ITS TRUST

- ✪ Start by having your chinchilla sit on the upturned palm of your hand when it is in its cage.

- ✪ When it is sitting on the upturned palm of your hand, gently lift it toward the cage door.

- ✪ At first it may jump off your hand, and you will have to start all over again.

When it does let you lift it out of its cage, you will know that your chinchilla considers you a friend.

Chinchillas love to have their chins and necks stroked and tickled.

Always hold your chinchilla's tail at the end nearest to its bottom. If you don't, you could damage it.

TAIL ALERT!

Never try to catch your chinchilla by grabbing at its tail. You will probably find that it will escape, and you will be left with just a small piece of tail fur in your hand!

Out of the cage

When holding your chinchilla, whether it is sitting on your hand or resting on your forearm, if you want to stop it from getting away, you can gently hold onto its tail (see picture above).

It is important when holding your pet that you don't squeeze it tightly. It won't like this and will try to get away if you are rough with it. It may even nip or bite you.

When holding your chinchilla, you must always be gentle and very patient.

SAFETY FIRST

If your chinchilla nips or scratches you, tell an adult. You should wash the bite or scratch with some cotton balls dipped in mild antiseptic. If the bite goes through your skin, you should be seen by your doctor.

Exercise time

Try to set aside some time every day for your pet to play outside its cage. While your chinchilla is running around, make sure you stay with it all the time, so it cannot get into trouble or get lost. Your chinchilla will like to race around the edges of your room, next to the walls, so try to create a clear path for your pet.

Make sure your pet cannot nibble any plants. They may be poisonous!

PREPARING YOUR ROOM

Your chinchilla will love exploring, but before you let it out of its cage, you will need to prepare for its exercise time.

- ✪ Make sure there are no open windows that your chinchilla could climb out of.

- ✪ Block up any holes that your pet might be tempted to investigate.

- ✪ Make sure there are no buckets of water or toilets that your pet can fall into. Chinchillas cannot swim. Their fur will get waterlogged and they will quickly drown.

- ✪ Keep electric cables out of reach of your pet. Chinchillas can gnaw through cables very easily so, to be extra careful, turn off any electrical equipment in the room.

- ✪ Remove any precious objects or things that would be bad for your chinchilla to chew on.

- ✪ If you have cats or dogs, put them in another room. They will frighten your chinchilla.

It is a good idea to stay with your pet all the time so that it cannot get into trouble or get lost.

Catching your chinchilla

Sometimes your chinchilla will not come to you when you want to put it back in its cage. If this happens, try to block off a small section of the room. Then offer your pet the palm of your hand so that it can step onto it. You may need to tempt your chinchilla with a single raisin to encourage it to step onto your hand.

If your chinchilla still refuses to come to you, place a carrying cage on the floor next to a straight part of the wall. Now guide your pet into it, using a piece of cardboard or plywood to form a path to the door of the carrying cage.

If your pet does not want to be picked up, it may help to offer it a small treat. Never grab your chinchilla. You will only frighten it.

Some Health Problems

Chinchillas rarely suffer from illnesses and diseases. However, here are a few of the problems that could affect your chinchilla's health.

Upset stomach

If your chinchilla's droppings are small, runny, and wet, it has an upset stomach. This may be caused by moldy hay. Do not feed your pet any more hay for three to four days. Also, make certain that it has plenty of pellets to eat and fresh water to drink. It should recover in a few days, but if it does not, take it to the vet.

This chinchilla is obviously healthy and **alert.** If your chinchilla sits quietly in the corner of its cage and does not notice you, it may *be sick.*

Eye problems

Sometimes when chinchillas use their dust bath, they may get a little sand in one of their eyes. The eye may become sore and even close up. If this happens, bathe the eye gently with warm water. This should help to clear the eye. However, if some pus comes out, the eye has become infected and it should be seen by a vet.

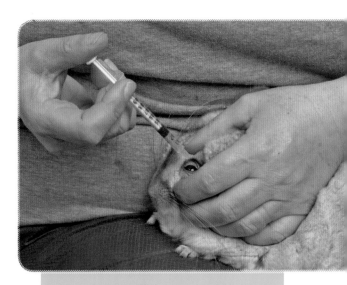

If your chinchilla's eye becomes infected, you should take it to a vet as soon as possible.

Cuts

Chinchillas rarely cut themselves. If your pet does get a small cut, call your vet for advice on how to care for the injury. Do not try to cover the wound with a bandage, because your pet will only chew it off. If your pet has a serious cut, you should take it to the vet immediately.

Heatstroke

If the temperature rises to 27°Celsius (80°Fahrenheit), it is too hot for your pet. If your chinchilla is suffering from too much heat, it will probably be lying down and breathing heavily and its ears will be bright pink or red. You must act quickly. If possible, take your pet to a cooler room. A fan can help to circulate the cooler air. Give it plenty of water to drink. If your chinchilla does not recover, contact the vet.

Chinchillas cannot take their fur coats off, so when the temperature rises they can get dangerously hot.

Fur fungus

Fur fungus is highly **contagious**. This means it can be passed on easily from one chinchilla to another. If you suspect that your chinchilla has fur fungus, you should **isolate** it immediately, keeping it away from other chinchillas.

A chinchilla with fur fungus will have bald patches on its body. The bald patches will be irritated and red and will look very sore. Usually the fungus starts around the nose, chin, eyes, ears, and tail. It is not a **fatal** disease, but it will make your chinchilla uncomfortable. Pets with fur fungus lose weight and can become bad tempered.

TOP TIP

⭐ If you suspect that your chinchilla has fur fungus, you should take it to the vet, who will give you advice on how to treat it.

⭐ In addition to treating your pet with ointment or medicine, you should also wash out its cage and all its equipment with hot, soapy water and a mild disinfectant. Rinse the cage thoroughly and make sure it is completely dry before putting your pet back in its cage.

If you are worried about your chinchilla's health, you should take it to the vet. You will need to transport your chinchilla in a suitable carrying cage. Make sure that it cannot chew its way out.

Fur chewing

You may notice that your chinchilla has started to chew its fur. No one knows for sure what causes fur chewing in chinchillas. Some people believe that chinchillas start biting their fur because they are nervous, because they do not have a well-balanced diet, or because they are not happy in the place that they are kept.

If your chinchilla starts biting its fur, try to think if something might be upsetting it. Perhaps you have changed its pellets or not given it hay every day. You may have changed the position of its cage so it no longer feels secure, or maybe it just wants more attention from you.

CATCHING CHINCHILLA DISEASES

Can humans catch chinchilla diseases from chinchillas? The answer is no—chinchillas have not been known to pass on any diseases to humans. However, you should always wash your hands after handling your chinchilla or cleaning its cage. You could get an upset stomach from touching its waste and droppings.

Some people think that chinchillas chew their fur because they are bored. Make sure your pet has plenty of toys to keep it occupied.

Visiting the Vet

Sometimes you will need to take your chinchilla to the vet. You should know your vet's address and telephone number in case of an emergency. These are some of the problems that your vet might need to deal with.

Tooth problems

Like all **rodents**, chinchillas have teeth that continue growing throughout their life. Rodents need to gnaw on things to stop their teeth from growing too long. However, even if you provide lots of chewing blocks for your chinchilla, it can still develop tooth problems.

The vet will need to give your pet a thorough physical examination.

WARNING SIGNS

These are some of the signs that your pet may have tooth trouble.

- ✪ Your chinchilla's **incisors** (front teeth) may be **overgrown** or may not be growing straight.

- ✪ Your pet may have runny eyes. It may be drooling from its mouth, down its neck and chest.

- ✪ It may be losing weight.

- ✪ It may be pawing at its mouth.

Malocclusion

If your pet is in obvious pain from a toothache, it may be suffering from **malocclusion**. This is a problem that happens when a chinchilla's teeth do not grow properly and, sadly, there is no cure for it. Animals with malocclusion can suffer badly. Their teeth can grow into their head or into the back of their eyes and jaws as well as into their mouth. They will have a very difficult time eating their pellets and hay.

If your pet develops malocclusion, you will need to see your vet. The vet may recommend that the chinchilla be **put down**. Although this will be sad for you, it is much better for your pet than letting it suffer. Happily, most chinchillas do not develop this problem.

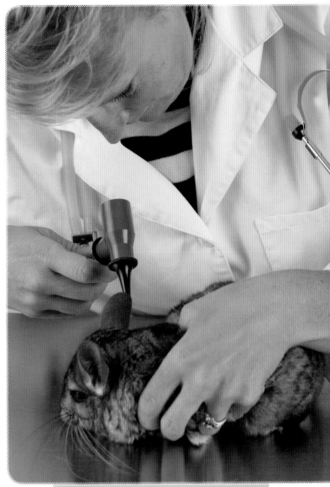

This vet has a special instrument that lets her see into the animal's ears.

Ear problems

If your chinchilla is constantly scratching its ears, this could be a sign of a problem developing. You should take your chinchilla to a vet. If your chinchilla has any obvious problems with its ears, such as a smelly **discharge** (liquid coming out of its ears) or wetness, you should contact your vet immediately. The vet may give you ear drops to put in your pet's ears or may suggest that you give it some **antibiotics** to clear up the problem.

Saying Goodbye

Some chinchillas can live for up to 20 years, but one day, no matter how well you care for your pet, it will die. Sometimes a chinchilla will die peacefully and unexpectedly. This will come as a shock to you, but do not blame yourself. There is probably nothing that you could have done.

When chinchillas get old, they become less energetic and spend more time sleeping. This chinchilla is old, but it is still in good condition.

A peaceful end

As a caring owner, the hardest responsibility of all is to know when to let your pet be **put down** to save it from suffering. Your chinchilla may be very old and in pain. Or it may have a serious illness that cannot be cured. Your vet will give it a small injection. This does not hurt—it just makes your pet sleepy. Before you can count to 10, your chinchilla will be asleep, and then its heart will stop beating. Your pet will appreciate it if you can cuddle it as it loses consciousness.

Feeling upset

No matter how it happens, you will feel upset when a pet dies, especially if your chinchilla has been a friend for many years. It is perfectly normal for people, adults as well as children, to cry when a pet dies or when they think of a dead pet.

Sometimes it helps to have a special burial place for your pet. You could plant a flower or a shrub on it to mark the spot. Eventually, the pain of losing your pet will pass, and you will be left with happy memories of your chinchilla.

Caring for your chinchilla will have taught you a lot about these lovable animals. Maybe you will be able to give a home to another chinchilla that needs love and care.

Keeping a Record

It is fun to keep a record of your chinchilla. Buy a big scrapbook and fill it with notes and photos. Then you can look back at all the things you and your pet did together. Your chinchilla scrapbook can include information that you might need when you take your pet to the vet or if you enter your pet in chinchilla shows.

You can take photos of your pet doing all sorts of things and then choose the best ones to put in your scrapbook.

A special diary

You could start your scrapbook with the first day that you saw your pet, whom you bought it from, and how old it was. You can write down special events in the life of your pet, such as the first time you saw it take a dust bath, the first day it sat on your lap or on your shoulders, and the first time you tried to **groom** it. You can make a note of the funny things your chinchilla does. If you enter your chinchilla into shows, you could write about the shows you go to—and the prizes it wins!

If you care for your chinchilla properly, you will both have a lot of fun together!

Useful information

If you bought your chinchilla from a **breeder**, you may have a **pedigree** document, with details of its mother and father. Your breeder may also tell you about members of your pet's family that won ribbons or awards. This is all good information to put in your scrapbook.

You might decide to collect magazine articles about chinchillas. Cut them out and keep them in your scrapbook. They will soon build up into a good source for tips and guidance.

CHINCHILLA SHOWS

Some people take their chinchillas to shows.

- Shows are held throughout the United States, Great Britain, Canada, Australia, and Europe.

- Judges decide which chinchillas are in the best condition and have the best shape and fur.

- There are groups that specialize in show-quality chinchillas. You can find details about these groups on page 47.

Glossary

alert lively and interested in everything

allergy sensitive reaction to something, which can make your skin itch or make you sneeze

antibiotics medicine that fights infection

breed keep animals and encourage them to mate so they produce young

breeder someone who owns animals and encourages them to mate and produce young

contagious passed on by touching or coming into close contact with something

cylindrical shaped like a tube or a cylinder

deformed crooked or bent out of shape

discharge liquid coming out of somewhere, such as an animal's ear

fatal deadly

galvanize treat to prevent rust

groom clean an animal's coat by brushing or combing it. Animals often groom themselves.

incisors front teeth

isolate keep apart from other animals or humans

kit young chinchilla

litter group of baby chinchillas born together

malocclusion disease that prevents teeth from growing straight

mammal animal with fur or hair on its body that feeds its babies with milk

molt lose fur at particular times of the year, usually spring or summer

nocturnal active at night

overgrown grown too long

pedigree document giving the names of an animal's parents

put down give a sick animal an injection to help it die peacefully and without pain

rodent animal with strong front teeth for gnawing

roughage food that takes a long time to digest and helps people and animals to stay healthy

selective breeding choosing animals with certain features such as fur color to mate together, so that their young also show those features

suckle drink milk from a mother

urine liquid passed out of the body containing water and waste substances

vitamin important substance found in food that helps people and animals to stay healthy

volcanic from an area with volcanoes

warm-blooded able to create body heat

wean become ready to eat solid food and stop drinking a mother's milk

Find Out More

Books

This is a list of books about chinchillas for adults. Most of them are simple guides that an adult can help you read:

Alderton, David. *Chinchillas*. Neptune City, N.J.: T. F. H., 2007.

Bartl, Juliana. *Chinchillas*. Hauppauge, N.Y.: Barron's, 2010.

Vanderlip, Sharon Lynn. *The Chinchilla Handbook*. Hauppauge, N.Y.: Barron's, 2006.

Websites

www.chinchillaclub.com
This Chinchilla Club website provides lots of information about owning chinchillas. The club also publishes a magazine.

www.echinchilla.com
This website contains lots of information about caring for chinchillas.

Groups

In addition to the Chinchilla Club, there are also smaller local clubs. Look for their address in your telephone book or in your local library. You could also ask your vet or your pet store owner about a local chinchilla club.

Index